THE
COTSWOLD
COLLECTION

This book is dedicated to Andrew Dawkes, Cotswold garden designer of great vision and empathy.

First published in the United Kingdom in 2010, this the Third Edition in 2019 by: Goldeneye, Penryn TR10 8JL

PHOTOGRAPHY: William Fricker
TEXT: William Fricker

Photographs copyright ©William Fricker, 2019
Text copyright ©William Fricker, 2019
Map copyright ©Goldeneye, 2019

DESIGNED BY: Flora Fricker

COVER IMAGE: Arlington Row, Bibury
BACK COVER IMAGE: View from Coaley Peak
& Cotswold Poppies

Printed in the EEC
ISBN Number: 9 78185965 261 9

All Rights Reserved

GOLDENEYE

goldeneyeguides.co.uk

The Glebe, Bourton-On-The-Water

CAPTURING THE PERFECT IMAGE — IS NEVER EASY

This book of photographic images is a testament to my long relationship with the Cotswolds—my base for thirty years.

For many of those years I walked, drove and cycled around the area researching and photographing for Goldeneye Guides. I played cricket in many of the villages and visited many hostelries. I married Caroline who had been brought up in Little Rissington and Guiting Power. My Mother, and Father-In-Law (for whom this book is dedicated) still live in the Cotswolds providing us with an ongoing base. I have come to know the area intimately and have developed a great love for the villages and rolling hills.

The mass use of cameras within digital apparatus creates the impression that photography is an easy craft. I still believe photography to be a difficult craft to master. No matter that one can now edit as one goes along, one still has to plan well in advance. Knowledge of your subject, the weather and where the sun rises or falls remains of importance. For example, the Arlington Row image on pages 62–63 took three years to plan for the sun only shines on the front of it for 10 minutes at a certain time of year. The image opposite of North Nibley's trees was a lucky shot, an unexpected bonus that rarely happens. I needed to shoot the Tyndale Monument before I returned home and the weather was lousy—fog, rain and cold. Walking up that steep path took me by surprise and my was I in luck. Earlier in the same week I had arrived at Westonbirt Arboretum to find the carpark overflowing. I nearly turned away. Luckily I didn't for the image of the swaying Acers was a pic I took when the area had cleared of visitors—My patience was justified.

I don't believe your camera equipment is that important. I just so happen to use Nikon. Starting with the Nikon FE and now the Nikon D800. Luckily, my old lenses are compatible with the later models. I am from the school of 'natural photography'. My intent has always been to represent my subject in the best possible light and from a perspective that you the reader of my books and guides can recognise. I admire those who can create amazing artistic imagery. That has never been my style. I hope that you find enjoyment and perhaps a little inspiration from the images in this book.

—*William Fricker, Cheltenham, May 2019*

North Nibley Trees

Windrush Cottage Garden

AN INTRODUCTION

What and where is the region known as the Cotswolds?
To those who know it, this may seem like a silly question. However, it is a place that manifests itself in many different ways to different people. Even down to the area they would define as the Cotswolds on a map. To some fashionistas, and magazine editors, the Cotswolds runs comparison to the New York Hamptons and Tuscany. Whilst to others the name is synonymous with wool and hunting, stone walls and majestic churches. From my point of view and for the purposes of this book, the area stretches from Chipping Campden in the north to Bath in the south, and from Gloucester to Witney, west to east. The book also features Oxford (because the building's materials are cut from Cotswold limestone) although it is not technically considered part of the Cotswolds.

The Cotswolds derives its name from two Saxon words: *"Cote"* – sheep fold, and *"Wold"* – bare hill. This references the importance of sheep in the development of the area. And, it is to the Cotswold Lion sheep that one must look for the origin of wealth and endeavour that brought prosperity to this region.

The Cotswolds region is perched on the central section of a ridge of Oolitic Limestone. The geological structure has thus had a profound and lasting affect on the landscape, and look of the area. The Oolitic Limestone that forms these hills has the appearance of thousands of tiny balls, like fish roe and is between 200 and 175 million years old. This ridge has been tilted on its side and is run off with streams and river valleys that lead off in a south-easterly direction to feed the Thames basin. On the western edge the scarp is steep in places with outcrops of rounded hills, notably Cam Long Down and Bredon Hill and makes for fine walking country and pleasing views across to the Malvern Hills and Wales.

Neolithic Man found refuge on these hills from the swamps of the Severn and Thames flood plains. The Celtic Dobunni tribe established hill forts where they farmed, bartered their crafts and founded coinage before the Romans arrived. They were not a warlike tribe like their neighbours the Silurians (Welsh) and eased into a compatible relationship with the conquering Romans to build Corinium Dobunnorum (Cirencester) into the second largest Roman settlement in Britain with a populace of 12,000 inhabitants.

The Saxon farmer laid the foundations of prosperity for the medieval wool merchants, and it was these merchants who built the great *"Wool"* churches and the great manor houses. More latterly, the Cotswolds has come to represent elegance and wealth. In the C18, Bath and Cheltenham epitomised the elegance, hedonism and splendour of the Georgian era.

The landscape is rich in imagery: dry-stone walls divide the vast, sweeping sheep pastures and lazy, winding, trout streams meander through the rich pastureland. Scattered across this landscape you will come across quaint hamlets undisturbed by coach, sightseer or time itself. All this makes for an idyllic scene, rarely bettered in England.

Saxton's Map – 1576
(Printed with the kind permission of the British Museum)

CONTENTS

BATH

Bath owes its fame to the discovery of hot springs in 863 BC. The Bath Springs were developed in about 60–70 AD by the Romans who built a wall around the 23 acre site naming it Aquae Sulis. It prospered for 400 years until the Romans withdrew from Britain in 410 AD. The city saw much prosperity in the Middle Ages from the sale of Cotswold wool. But the heyday of Bath began over a 40 year period when three men of immense vision transformed the city with a populace of 3,000 into the Georgian city of 30,000 citizens. They were Beau Nash (Master of Ceremonies, manners and fashion), John Wood, (architect), and Ralph Allen, (benefactor, financier and quarry owner who supplied the building materials). In a city of such architectural beauty, of particular note are The Circus and The Royal Crescent.

Originally named King's Circus, The Circus was the vision of John Wood the Elder and was built between 1754 and 1768. It was his intention to create a classical Palladian architectural landscape inspired by Rome's Colosseum. The Circus is made up of 33 terraced houses. Thomas Gainsborough lived in No.17 from 1765–1774. On the architect's death, The Circus was completed by his son, John Wood the Younger. The Royal Crescent was also built by him, between 1767 and 1774. Today the 30 original homes are split into flats, houses and a hotel, and many are privately owned.

The Circus

The River Avon, Pulteney Bridge

BATH ABBEY

The Church of St Peter and St Paul, otherwise known as Bath Abbey, has been the home of three churches: an Anglo-Saxon church in 757 and a Norman Cathedral in 1090 but later in 1137 much of this was destroyed by fire.

Today's building was founded in 1499 to replace the ruin damaged in the fire. But again it had to be rebuilt in 1611 following Henry VIII's Dissolution of the Monasteries. In simple architectural terms it can be described as Perpendicular Gothic and cruciform in plan. The fan vaulting of the Nave is very fine and was designed by Robert and William Vertue, designers of Henry VII's chapel in Westminster Abbey. It was never finished until Gilbert Scott completed the original designs in the 1860's. Note the Stairway to Heaven on the West Front.

Bath Abbey & Roman Baths

◀ The Royal Crescent   ▲ Abbey Green

BRADFORD ON-AVON

A few minutes train ride from Bath but a world away given the few tourists who tramp her streets. This market town is a gem.

The narrow streets are lined with independent shops often set within an impressive array of medieval and Georgian architecture. Buildings hug the hillside and tumble almost accidentally into the River Avon. As one walks about one is constantly reminded of the towns historic past for the eye is always catching the sight of weaver's cottages scattered hither and thither in their many shapes and sizes built in Cotswold stone. There is much to see.

Overlooking the River Avon is Abbey Mill. Built in the mid-1800s for use as a cloth mill. Today it has been converted into flats. The Town Bridge was originally built by the Normans and on it stands The Blind House, where local drunks and troublemakers were locked up. To realise the ancient history of this town just visit the Saxon Church of St Laurence formerly a monastery in the C7.

The photographs here illustrate The Chantry once the home of successful clothiers. The Town Bridge and The Blind House described above, and cottages overlooking Barton Steps which lead down to the back of The Chantry. On the other side of town you have the Tithe Barn, formerly part of the estate of Shaftesbury Abbey, the C14 barn was used to collect "tithes" or income in the form of produce, and livestock, for the Abbey. The barn is 51 metres (168ft) long and has a spectacular timber-cruck roof. One of the largest stone roofs in Europe.

◀ The Chantry　　▲ The Town Bridge / Barton Steps

CASTLE COMBE

One of the prettiest, and most visited villages in the south Cotswolds lies sheltered in a hidden valley surrounded by steep, wooded hills.

In former times, a flourishing medieval wool centre, as evidenced by the weavers and clothiers cottages that descend from the Market Cross to By Brook, and the three-arch bridge. Its great claim to fame followed its appearance in the 1966 film of *Doctor Doolittle* starring Rex Harrison. The village remains a popular location for TV commercials, and period dramas, because of its rows of quaint cottages undisturbed by time, or any life. More recently, used in Stephen Spielberg's 2011 film *War Horse*.

◀ Footpath above Colham Wood & By Brook   ▲ Weavers Cottages

LACOCK

This is a show village owned and protected by the National Trust. You could be forgiven for thinking you were on a film set. Not surprisingly, it is a favourite for location scouts. *Pride and Prejudice*, *Cranford* and *Wolfman* are just some of the TV/Film productions made here. The houses are lime-washed and half-timbered, and many date from the C13. There are some old inns and tearooms, and gift shops awaiting your custom.

◀ Town House, Lacock   ▲ Lacock Abbey

MALMESBURY ABBEY

Founded as a Benedictine Monastery in 676 AD by the saintly and scholarly Brother Aldhelm. King Athelstan was buried here in 941 AD. By the C11 the monastery held the second largest library in Europe and was a place of learning and pilgrimage. The Abbey was built and completed by 1180. The tall spire rose to 431 feet (131m) and was to be seen for miles around. However, in 1500 it collapsed destroying the Nave and the Transept.

A few years later, in 1550, the West Tower also col-

lapsed. What you see today is less than half of the original structure. Yet, it still remains a formidable church and a sight to behold. It was also a place of great inspiration for in 1010 the monk Eilmer of Malmesbury became the first (recorded) man to fly by jumping off the roof of the Tower and to fly his hang glider 200 yards before crashing and breaking both his legs—Leonardo da Vinci was to design a similar machine 350-years later!

◄ Tombstones, Malmesbury Abbey   ▲ Entrance to Abbey

WESTONBIRT ARBORETUM

If you believe trees to be the most beautiful things in creation then a visit to this arboreal wonderland must be at the top of your agenda.

Here, in this paradise garden, you will find 600 acres of magnificent trees and shrubs from around the world. With no less than 15,500 individual specimens of 3,000 different tree types, and a good 17 miles of footpaths ahead you will need comfy footwear. Needless to say, it is quite a sight in Spring and Autumn, and popular, too. Award-winning Canopy Treetop Walkway accessible for all leading into Silk Wood area. On arrival you are greeted by the beautiful timber-built Welcome Building and Visitor Centre. Westonbirt Restaurant is open every day with Courtyard Café open for snacks and hot drinks at busy times. Shop opens every day for books and gifts. See website for opening times and prices.

◀ Yellow and Gold Acers   ▶ Red Acers in the Wind

THE COTSWOLD WAY

A magical long distance footpath covering over 100 miles from Chipping Campden to Bath. It follows the edge of the escarpment, meanders through picturesque villages, past pre-historic sites and provides spectacular views usually westward towards the Malvern Hills and Wales. It is signposted.

For short excursions set out from Cleeve Hill, Winchcombe, Broadway, Painswick, Coaley Peak and Wotton-Under-Edge.

You are never far from civilisation. The tea rooms and inns are often a welcome refuge. The hardy and fit will cover the distance in four or five days. The average walker will require a good week. Beware of mud and short, sharp ascents.

▲ Below Coaley Peak
◄ Broadway Tower Country Park / Nibley Knoll

34   Devil's Chimney, Leckhampton Hill

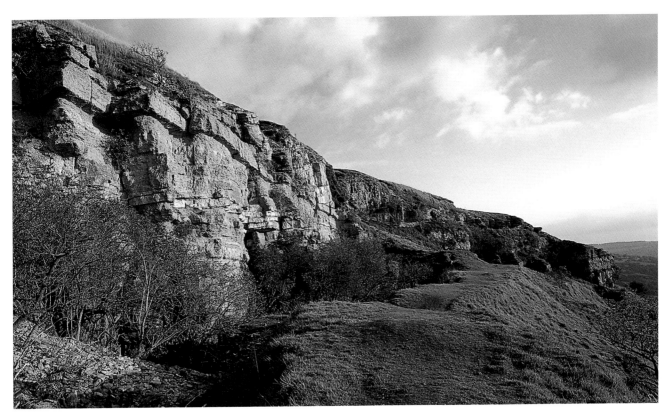

Cleeve Cloud, Cleeve Hill, Cheltenham / View from Haresfield Beacon

PAINSWICK

Its local description as *"The Queen of the Cotswolds"* is fully justified. The houses and cottages are built from a grey, almost white, limestone, in marked contrast to Broadway and Chipping Campden, and some of the buildings have an almost Palladian, statuesque quality about them.

Look out for the Court House and The Painswick (hotel). Wander down the pretty side streets, but

above all, you must, and it's tricky to ignore, visit the churchyard famous for the legendary 99 yew trees. The 100th yew tree has been planted, time and again, but has never survived. Painswick is one of the gems of the southern Cotswolds, and is a worthy base from which to explore this region. It is also connected to a network of footpaths including the Cotswold Way, so you can arrive by car, or taxi, and then just walk for the rest of your stay.

Three Views of Painswick Churchyard

Bibury Cottage

Great Tew Cottage

Windrush Cottage

LAURIE LEE COUNTRY

Laurie Lee, 1914–1997, was an Author, Film Maker, Musician, Novelist, Playwright, Poet, Screenwriter and Travel Writer. He was born in Stroud and brought up in the village of Slad. His family came from nearby Sheepscombe. Laurie is remembered for his autobiographical trilogy *Cider With Rosie* (1959), *As I Walked Out One Midsummer Morning* (1969), and *A Moment of War* (1991).

Cider With Rosie established him as a brilliant and original writer of descriptive prose. It's an achingly evocative chronicle of village life before the advent of the motor car and an English countryside lost in time. It has sold in excess of six million copies worldwide. Laurie was a slow ponderous writer who debated over every syllable and word. He spent most of his life in Chelsea but would often return to Slad and wander up and around the valleys close to his cottage.

He was most proud of his poetry. His first volume, *The Sun My Monument* was published in 1944. His last Selected Poems in 1983. He lies buried in Slad's Churchyard overlooking his beloved Woolpack Inn.

View Across Fields to Slad

Down Wood

Cranham Woods

Saltridge Woods

View from the Woolpack Inn

THE DUNTISBOURNES

A group of isolated hamlets, perhaps described as a string of four villages dotted along a beautiful valley. Time stands still here. For those seeking an England of ancient churches, rose covered cottages and the sound of the sky lark, none better. Duntisbourne Abbots stands at the head of the valley and is the largest of them. The road to Duntisbourne Leer runs adjacent to the stream, the Dunt Brook flowing through each hamlet. Middle Duntisbourne and Duntisbourne Rouse are two farming hamlets, the latter famous for its idyllic Saxon church.

▲ **Duntisbourne Abbots Churchyard**

◀ **Duntisbourne Rouse Church**

◀ **Middle Duntisbourne Barns**

OWLPEN

An iconic group of picturesque Cotswold buildings: Manor House, Tithe Barn, Church, Mill and Court House. Water Garden and terrace. The Tudor manor dates from 1450–1616 but the whole estate has 900 years of history to tell.

CHAVENAGE

A haunted Elizabethan manor house that has remained virtually unchanged for 400 years. A replica of a bygone age. It contains two complete tapestry rooms, furniture and relics of the Civil War. Guided tours by the Lowsley-Williams family. Location as George and Elizabeth War-leggan's home in the current *Poldark* TV series.

CIRENCESTER

One of the finest and most affluent towns in the Cotswolds lies surrounded by a plethora of attractive villages whose populace (often second home owners) tend to shop and hobnob in Ciren (as the locals call it). The smart shops and bars reflect the riches of its patrons. As the Roman town Corinium, it became the second largest Roman town (after London) in Britain. Its strategic position at the confluence of the major routes (the Fosse Way, Ermin Way and Akeman Street) combined with the vast rolling sheep pastures brought great wealth in the Middle Ages.

◀ Parish Church of St John the Baptist   ▲ Roman Carving, Corinium Museum

Cirencester

THE COTSWOLD HORSE

The horse, Equus ferus caballus, has evolved over 45–55 million years. They began to be domesticated about 4,000 BC and by 2,000 BC their use had spread across much of Europe, Central Asia and the Middle East. The only wild horse still in existence is the Przewalski, of Mongolian origin and now a protected species.

To many who live in the Cotswolds the horse is synonymous with their lifestyle. Whether it be hunting with hounds, training hunters for racing, point-to-pointing, playing polo, running a livery stable or just owning a horse for the simple pleasure of exercise, and because you adore these beautiful creatures. You can't travel very far in the Cotswolds without coming across a horse being ridden down a country lane or seeing ponies chasing each other around a field. The Cotswold countryside is criss-crossed with hundreds of miles of bridleways. For starters, you could try the Sabrina Way, a 44 mile (70km) route from Forthampton to Great Barrington. For details of more routes go to: *ride-uk.org.uk* For those wishing to join this merry band there are many riding stables just itching to teach you.

The Cotswold calendar is choc-a-bloc with events: from Cheltenham's *National Hunt festival* in March, to the *Badminton Horse Trials* in May, to the *Gatcombe Park festival* in August. In between are point-to-points, pony club meets and hunts.

▲ Stow Horse Fair / Cirencester Polo Club
◀ Andoversford Point-to-Point / Cirencester Park

BARNSLEY HOUSE GARDENS

The former home of the garden expert, the late Rosemary Verey. A chic hotel and spa offering discreet and friendly service, great food and state-of-the-art technology. A visit to this extraordinary garden may cost you lunch, but it will be a worthwhile, and memorable experience. Make sure you visit the vegetable garden.

BAUNTON CHURCH

St Christopher Wallpainting, Church of St Mary Magdalene, Baunton. This is a 15th century work of art depicting St Christopher carrying the Christ child across a stream.

It has recently been restored. The Norman Church was built by the Augustinian monks from Cirencester Abbey as a Chapel of Ease in 1150.

Coln Rogers

Life on the River Coln, Bibury

BIBURY

William Morris described Bibury as *"One of the prettiest villages in England"*, and few would argue with him. As a honey-pot village made up of rose-covered cottages set behind idyllic kitchen gardens it attracts the crowds. Running parallel to the pavement is the River Coln inhabited by swans, ducklings and trout. During the C17 Bibury was notorious as a buccaneering centre for gambling and horse racing that took place on the Macaroni Downs near Eastleach. All visitors to Bibury are drawn to admire Arlington Row, the iconic cottages that were originally monastic wool barns. In the C17 they were converted into weavers' homes. Now domestic dwellings they overlook Rack Isle, a four-acre water meadow where cloth was once hung out to dry.

◀ Cottage Garden, Bibury   ▲ Rose Cottage, Arlingham

Arlington Row

EASTLEACH

The twin hamlets of Eastleach Turville and Eastleach Martin face each other across the River Leach. The ancient clapper bridge (Keble's Bridge) connects the two. This was most likely built by the Keble family whose descendant, John Keble, was curate here in 1815. He founded the Oxford Movement and is known for his volume of religious verse *The Christian Year.*

Across the river the tiny church of St Andrews hidden beneath the trees and which has a more interesting interior than its neighbour. Note, the splendid C14 saddleback tower of a Transitional, and early English period style. A Norman doorway C.1130 with a carved Tympanum of Christ. To the west is Macaroni Downs where the rolling sheep pastures were once the location for Regency derring-do, gambling and horse racing. Now just munched by sheep, cattle and ridden through by mountain bikers. For refreshments there is the Victoria Inn, and for more sophisticated fare, The Swan at Southrop.

▲ Macaroni Downs
◀ Kebles Bridge
◀ Daffodil Walk & Kebles Bridge

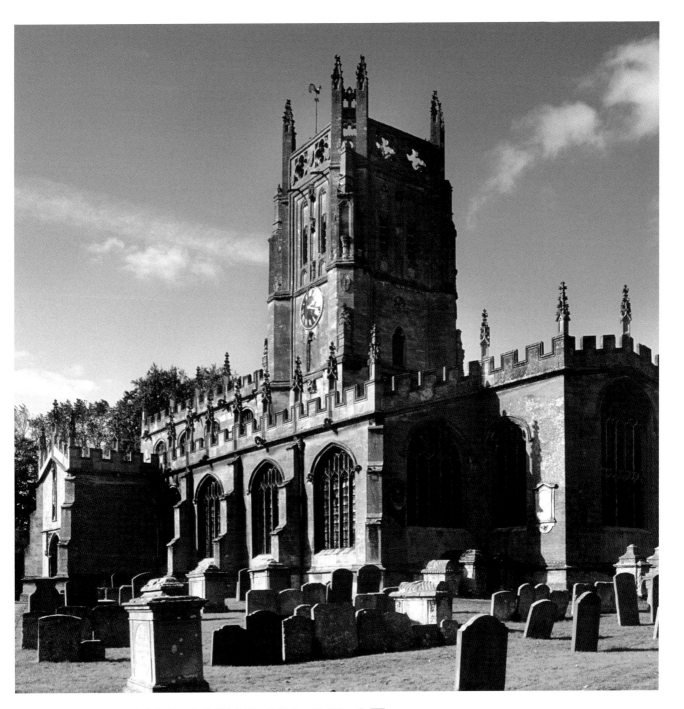

THE PARISH CHURCH OF ST MARY THE VIRGIN, FAIRFORD

This perfect, late C15 Perpendicular church is world-famous for the outstanding 28 stained glass windows depicting scenes from Genesis to the Last Judgement. Of further interest are the carved misericords and recumbent brasses, and the C6 Saxon cemetery. Set in an attractive market town on the tranquil River Coln.

BOURTON-ON-THE-WATER

One of the most popular beauty spots in the Cotswolds but best visited out of season or at daybreak. It can be charming on a quiet, frost-bitten morning when only the postman is out and about so be advised to avoid a busy bank holiday when the hordes arrive in coaches and their charabancs. With ice cream in hand the visitors sit beside the river wetting their bare feet in the Windrush, and there's not a stitch of green grass visible through all the paraphernalia. The tourist brochures describe it as *"The Venice of the Cotswolds"*, because the River Windrush is spanned with low grace-ful bridges.

You must, however, look beyond the crowds and the gift shops and wander the lit-tle streets for there are some beautiful houses to admire. Bourton may not thrill the jaded teenager or hard-bitten traveller, but it will delight small children who love to run across the little bridges, paddle in the river and feed the ducks, and you have, of course, Birdland, the Model Village, the Motoring Museum and the Model Railway, all devised for family fun and rainy days. The village is built above Salmonsbury Camp, a Roman settlement, and also above a former underground reservoir.

Secret Garden, The Glebe, Bourton-on-the-Water

Secret Garden, The Glebe, Bourton-on-the-Water

NORTHLEACH & SURROUNDS

Northleach is a village notable for its exceptional 15th century church with a South Porch described as the most lovely in all of England. It has tall pinnacles and state filled niches and some interesting monuments. The Market Place hosts farm shops and oversees various eateries. Nearby, across the fields is the ancient hamlet of Hampnett. With Old Manor and Church, and many an ancient burial site,

its history is long and uneven. To the south-east of the village, the isolated Lodge Park. A 'little' property with a big (boozy) history. A grandstand (folly) built by John 'Crump' Dutton in 1634 so he could watch deer coursing in comfort and share his passion for gambling, drinking and wenching.

◀ **Church of St Peter & St Paul, Northleach / Lodge Park**   ▲ **Hampnett**

COTSWOLD FARM PARK

A unique survival centre for rare historic breeds of British farm animals including the Cotswold Lions (the Golden Fleece), lies elevated, high on the Central Wolds, three miles from Bourton. Pets and tots corner. Farm trail.

Lambing, shearing and seasonal exhibitions. The recent popularity of the Farm Park has been in no small measure due to appearing on BBC TVs Country File.

◀ Cotswold Lions   ▲ Sow & Piglets

CHEDWORTH ROMAN VILLA

Discovered in 1864 by a local gamekeeper and later excavated
between 1864 and 1866 revealing remains of a Romano–British
villa containing mosaics, baths and hypocausts.

◄ Fairford Stained Glass   ▲ Mosaic, Chedworth Roman Villa

Guiting Power

GUITING POWER

A hidden, somnolent estate village that surprisingly manages to support two inns, a village shop/tea room and a bakery, a nursery school and an active Village Hall with children's playground. The blue-grey cottages belong to the Cochrane Estate (or Guiting Manor Amenity Trust) that has thankfully saved this village from greedy developers and second homers. The Church of St Michael & All Angels lies on the edge of the village and has some Norman features, a beautiful Tympanum and some weather-beaten tombstones. It was an early Anglo-Saxon settlement called Gyting Broc. A classical, blues and jazz music festival is held in late July these past 50 years and attracts many artists of international renown. Off the beaten track and worthy of a visit for those seeking a short circular walk and a piece of Cotswold heaven.

◀ Guiting Church / It's A Dog's Life　　▲ Church of St Michael & All Angels

Rose Cottage, Guiting Power

THE SLAUGHTERS

Lower Slaughter is one of the most popular villages in the Cotswolds. Little bridges cross the Eye Stream which runs beside rows of golden cottages. The much painted C19 red-brick Corn Mill, the Old Mill Museum, stands on the western edge of the village. This has been lovingly restored into a small museum with ice cream parlour, tea room and mill shop. The proprietor is the lead singer in a Jazz band, hence the funky music.

For those seeking a bed for the night there is first the Lower Slaughter Manor. A hotel with old-fashioned virtues set in a perfectly proportioned C17 Cotswold manor house. The rooms are spacious and decorated in the classical style with antiques. Across the road is the Slaughters Country Inn. A hostelry with a pleasing mix of contemporary and historic features.

Upper Slaughter is a couple of miles upstream and has an old Manor House once lived in by the Slaughter family, an old Post Office with a beautiful kitchen garden and along a lane past the church, a ford crosses the stream hidden beneath lush greenery. You also have the Lords of the Manor, a classy, well established country house hotel with C17 origins set in 8 acres of parkland. Child friendly. No dogs. The former home of the Reverend F.E.B Witts, Rector of this parish who wrote his famous chronicle of the C18, *The Diary of a Cotswold Parson.*

Entrance to Lower Slaughter

Lower Slaughter

CERNEY HOUSE GARDENS

Just look around, and you will surmise that this garden has been created by persons of immense enthusiasm, passion and experimentation. And, you have a garden of maturity, with old roses and herbaceous borders that sit well beside the walled kitchen-flower garden. You may purchase plants from their expansive plant collections.

BOURTON HOUSE GARDEN

This property was acquired by the Paices in 1983. For the next 25 years they transformed the neglected garden into the beautiful garden you see today. This garden occupies 3 acres of intense planting; topiary, knot garden, potager and a profusion of herbaceous borders and exotic plants. Parallel to this is the 7 acre walled pasture given over to specimen trees.

The wonderful C16 tithe barn is host to a gallery of contemporary arts and crafts, lunches and teas. The house was rebuilt as a four square Jacobean house by the eminent lawyer, Sir Nicholas Overbury in 1598. Later in the C18 the house was rebuilt on an earlier footprint by Alexander Popham, the grandson of a Cromwellian general. Thereto, it was taken down to the ground floor but the whimsical towers remain. And, for the next three hundred years the house has remained as you see it today.

MORETON-IN-MARSH

The wide, main street built by the Abbot of Westminster in 1220 for the sheep and arable sales is today a lively scene on Tuesday market day. Its origins go back to the Romans who built a military camp around 43-50 AD whilst planning the construction of the Fosse Way. It remains the largest town in the North East Wolds and is dominated by the Market Hall built in 1887 by Lord Redesdale father of the infamous Mitford sisters.

STOW-ON-THE-WOLD

With a name like this it is bound to attract visitors, and it has, and does so to this day, for with its exposed position at the intersection of eight roads (one being the Fosse Way) Stow has been party to some momentous events in history. The Romans used Stow as an encampment and route centre. The Viking merchants traded down the Fosse Way, but it was the Saxon hill farmers who laid the foundations for the fleece which created wealth for the wool merchants who used the great Market Place for sheep sales of 20,000 or more.

SUDELEY CASTLE

One of the great houses of Gloucestershire that was the original home of the Seymour family. Queen Katherine Parr, the last and surviving wife of Henry VIII lived here and lies buried in the Chapel. King Charles 1 found refuge here during the English Civil War when his nephew Prince Rupert set up camp here at the Castle. This irritated Cromwell who determined it should remain empty and so it lay neglected and derelict for nearly 200-years. Later bought by the Dent-Brocklehursts who made their wealth from glove-making.

The interior has a fine collection of needlework, furniture and many great master paintings. All surrounded by a breathtaking 1,200 acre estate and ten award-winning gardens, designed in part, by the late Rosemary Verey of Barnsley House. The centrepiece is the Queens Garden, named after four of England's queens: Anne Boleyn, Katherine Parr, Lady Jane Grey and Elizabeth 1 who so it is claimed walked upon the original Tudor Parterre.

Cotswold Lavender, Snowshill

GARGOYLES

The word gargoyle is a derivation from the French word gargouille meaning throat or pipe. Carved gargoyles were invented to channel water off, or away, from the roofs of buildings. The reason for the strange and often ugly designs is open to conjecture. Some believe they are caricatures of the clergy, or that they are there to ward off evil spirits. Others believe they are transformed into ghosts and ghoulies at night!

Gargoyles, Church of St Peter, Winchcombe

SNOWSHILL

This charming and unspoilt hilltop village is a short distance from Broadway. There is a striking church, a pub and a row of much photographed cottages opposite Snowshill Manor. Once home to the eccentric Charles Pagent Wade, it now houses some 22,000 items from his collection of toys, musical instruments, bicycles, clocks and samurai armour.

CHASTLETON HOUSE

A handsome Jacobean Manor built between 1607 and 1612 for Walter Jones who had made his fortune from the Law. His Welsh family had associations with the Wool Trade. The house has associations with the English Civil War and the Gunpowder Plot. The house retains its faded glory with a superb collection of tapestries, original furniture and ornamental topiary. The Long Gallery is almost unique with its barrel vaulted ceiling at a length of 72 feet. There are two croquet lawns on the middle terraces originally laid out by Walter Whitmore-Jones in the 1860s. His rules of the game were published in The Field in 1865 and thus Chastleton is considered the birthplace of croquet as a competitive sport. Don't miss the church next door.

BREDON HILL

A circumnavigation of Bredon Hill is a fine introduction to the beautiful villages of Kemerton, Overbury, Conderton, Ashton-under-Hill and Elmley Castle.

A lovely mix of Cotswold stone and black-and-white timbered buildings with many fine Inns and peaceful churchyards. Various footpaths lead up to the summit from Elmley and Kemerton. Superb views from this isolated limestone hill at 961ft. Over to Wales, the Vale of Evesham, the rivers Severn and Avon, and to the Cotswolds. Walk up to the Iron Age fort that is protected with two ramparts and the scene of a great battle at the time of Christ. It is believed the hostile tribe to have been Belgic invaders. Thereafter, the site was abandoned. The hacked remains of 50 men were found near the entrance many years later. It is one of the most important wildlife sites in England providing ancient woodland, calcareous grassland and scrub.

Bredon Hill features in many works by writers, poets and musicians. John Moore's *Brensham Trilogy* describes life in and about the hill. A.E. Housman's 1896 anthology, *A Shropshire Lad* has immortalised the hill and Ralph Vaughan Williams *Lark Ascending* may well have been inspired by his visits here.

STANWAY

This village is dominated by the outstanding Manor House. In its grounds stands one of the country's finest tithe barns designed with the Golden Proportion in mind and across the road a thatched cricket pavilion, set on staddle stones. The beautiful Gatehouse is C17, and was probably built by Timothy Strong of Little Barrington.

It bears the arms of the Tracy family. The little Church of St Peter has C14 origins and some amusing gargoyles. The restored C18 cascade (fountain) and canal in Stanway House was designed by the highly respected Charles Bridgman.

STANTON

A charming village with houses of warm honey-coloured jurassic limestone that was restored by Sir Philip Stott from 1903–37 who rescued the Estate from oblivion. A centre for equine excellence in the Vine—a popular horse riding centre. The Mount Inn is a welcome refuge if one's tackling the Cotswold Way.

COTSWOLD WOOLLEN WEAVERS

The story of wool and woollen cloth has woven its way into every fabric of Cotswold life, as has the stone that has built the barns, churches, manor houses and villages. The stone is brilliantly displayed by the masons' sculptures and workmanship. The cloth and the garments made up in their many guises (scarves, handbags, throws, jackets, skirts, coats, upholstery, as well as rolls of cloth) mirror the delights of this unique establishment.

▲ Stone Wall, Snowshill
◄ Cotswold Woollen Weavers, Filkins

CHELTENHAM

A smaller version of Bath, often described as *"the most complete Regency town in England"*. Elegant Regency buildings overlook the crescents, squares, tree-lined avenues and spacious parks.

Cheltenham remains, in historic terms, a young town of a mere 300-years. It grew as a spa after George III had approved the waters in 1788. Thereafter, distinguished visitors such as George Handel and Samuel Johnson came to be revitalised. The Promenade is one of the most attractive shopping streets in England which becomes progressively more independent and up-market as you head west towards Montpelier.

Cheltenham is proud of its calendar of cultural festivals: *Antique, Folk, Jazz, Literature, Music, Science,* but it is during the *Cheltenham Festival of National Hunt Racing* which takes place in March that the town takes on a carnival atmosphere. Horse Racing was introduced here in 1815 but it was not until 1902 that the *National Hunt Festival* was launched as we know it today.

The first British jet aircraft prototype, the Gloster E.28/29 was developed by the Gloster Aircraft Company at Hucclecote on the outskirts of Cheltenham. Built to Frank Whittle and George Carter's designs, this aircraft first flew in 1941. Their design contributed to the development of the Gloster Meteor, the first operational jet fighter to enter service with the Allies.

Suffolk Square

◀ Pittville Lawn   ▲ Pittville Park / Pittville Pump Room

GLOUCESTER

The county town of Gloucestershire was originally a port connected to the tidal Bristol Channel and a strategic point developed by the Romans into the fort Glevum. Today, it is not unusual to spy tall ships at the Old Docks where the spectacular C19 warehouses have been restored.

This ancient city is dominated by the magnificent Cathedral Church of St Peter, and the Holy and Undivided Trinity. Without exception the most magnificent building in Gloucestershire, and one of the finest of all English cathedrals. Its architecture is Romanesque, with some early Perpendicular. The East Window behind the altar had at its installation the largest display of medieval stained glass in the world and dates from 1350. The same year, fan vaulting was invented here at Gloucester and its intricate design covers the roof of the cloisters.

Statue of the Apostles, Gloucester Cathedral

130 **The Central Spire, Gloucester Cathedral**

The Cloisters Fan Vaulting / Tom Denny's Memorial Window to Gerald Finzi

TEWKESBURY

Founded in 1087 by the nobleman Robert Fitzhamon. However, the present building was started in 1102 to house Benedictine monks. The Norman Abbey was consecrated in 1121. The Nave and roof finished in the C14 in the Decorated style. Much is Early English and Perpendicular, although it is larger than many cathedrals and has according to Pevsner, *"the finest Romanesque Tower in England"*. The Abbey opens its doors to three major music festivals: *Musica Deo Sacra, the Three Choirs Festival* and the *Cheltenham Music Festival*.

◀ West Front, Tewkesbury Abbey   ▲ Abbey Fields in Flood

Tewkesbury

BROADWAY

"The Painted Lady of the Cotswolds", is a term often used to describe this beautiful village. The honey coloured stone captivates the visitor today as it did in the C19 when William Morris and his pre-Raphaelite friends settled here. A slow walk up the High Street will reveal some large and impressive houses that have been homes to Edward Elgar, J.M Barrie (Peter Pan), Ralph Vaughan Williams, Sir Gerald Navarro MP and Laura Ashley. Overlooked by Broadway Tower, an C18 folly tower and country retreat of William Morris. On a clear day 12 counties can be seen from the top of the Tower.

HIDCOTE MANOR GARDENS

One of the finest gardens of the C20 designed by Major Lawrence Johnston in the *"Arts & Crafts"* style. It is made up of garden rooms with rare trees, shrubs, herbaceous borders and *"old"* roses. The all weather court has recently been restored.

CHIPPING CAMPDEN

A perfect example of a Cotswold town, containing many ancient and remarkable buildings. The harmony of Cotswold stone mirrors the town's prosperity in the Middle Ages.

The Gabled Market Hall was built in 1627 by the wealthy landowner Sir Baptist Hicks whose mansion was burnt down in the Civil War, and the remains are the two lodges beside the Church. The Church of St James is a tall and statuesque *"Wool"* church. William Grevel, one of the wealthiest wool merchants, is remembered in the church on a brass transcription which reads: *"the flower of the wool merchants of all England"*. Opposite his house (Grevel's House) on the High Street is the Woolstaplers Hall, the meeting place for the fleece (staple) merchants.

Market Hall

144 ▲ Broad Campden in Frost ▶ Topiary Cottage, Chipping Campden

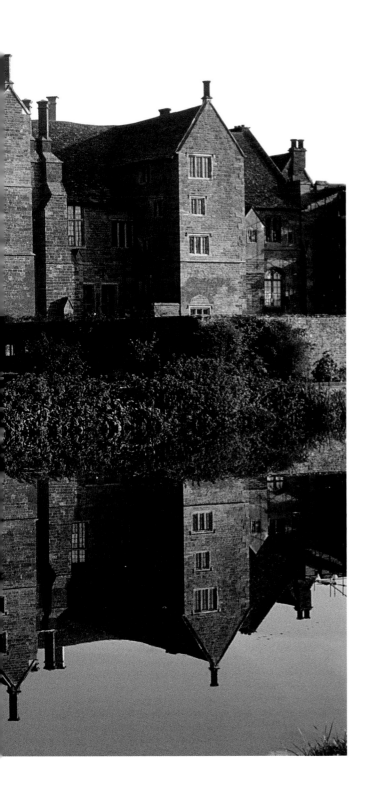

BROUGHTON CASTLE

Home to the Lords Saye and Sele (Fiennes family), for over 600 years. Originally, a moated medieval manor house that was substantially enlarged in the C16. The interior has a wealth of interest; magnificent plaster ceilings, fine panelling and fireplaces but it is to the exterior that one is drawn to—the reflections in the moat and the multi-coloured borders.

GREAT TEW

A sensationally beautiful village lined with ironstone cottages covered in thatch and stone tiles. Much of the village was designed by the Scottish architect John Claudius London. The Falkland Arms is named after Lord Falkland who lived here, and who died fighting for Charles I at the Battle of Newbury.

BURFORD

The first major Cotswold town you come to if travelling from the East. Burford has a picturesque, wide High Street, with classical gables atop some gracious houses, which slopes down to the dreamy River Windrush.

It's worth exploring the side streets, host to some splendid inns and pretty cottages and not to be missed, the fine Parish Church, notable for the intricately carved table tombs.

◄ Church of St John the Baptist / River Windrush

▲ The Tanfield Monument, Church of St John the Baptist

Burford Reflections

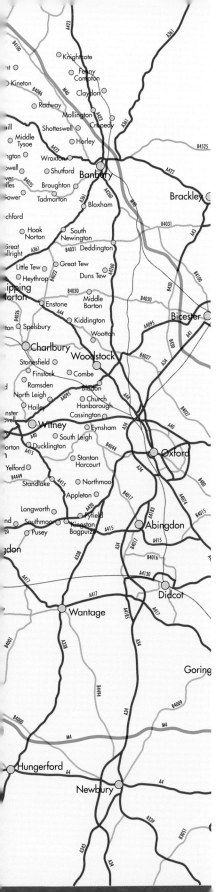

ACKNOWLEDGEMENTS...

This book is dedicated to my Father-In-Law, Andrew Dawkes, of The Glebe, Bourton-On-the-Water. Andrew is a true Man of the Cotswolds. He has lived in and around Bourton all his life. He has dedicated his life to designing and maintaining gardens of all sizes and structures sometimes over a period of ten to fifteen years. His way was not to redesign the wheel for his clients. He would gently suggest this and that and find that the client would suggest (off their own bat) one of his ideas to him a few days later. The hard work has taken its toll on his body and he is now facing retirement and rest from his labours. I wish him well and a long retirement.

I would like to thank the following for allowing me to photograph their properties: Barnsley House, Batsford Arboretum, Beaufort Polo Club, Broadway Tower Country Park, Burford Parish Church, Janet Angus of Cerney House Gardens, Chipping Campden Parish Church, Corinium Museum, The Earl of Wemyss and March of Stanway House, Fairford Parish Church, Gloucester Cathedral, Guiting Power Parish Church, Cotswold Farm Park, Lords Saye and Sele of Broughton Castle, Lowsley-Williams of Chavenage, Bourton House Garden, National Trust – Chedworth Roman Villa, Hidcote and Lacock Abbey, Manders of Owlpen Manor, Painswick Parish Church, Tewkesbury Abbey and Winchcombe Parish Church. And, not forgetting all those Cotswold folk who tend their cottage gardens and kindly allow me to record their labours.

My heartfelt thanks and love goes to my daughter Flora who has re-designed the layout of this book for the second time (in between her busy schedule). Her commitment to this project has been *"Beyond the Call..."* It has been a delight to call upon her services.

BIOGRAPHY

William Fricker was born in Somerset and educated at Stonyhurst College, Lancashire, and in various places of learning in Austria and Germany. He has worked in publishing for many years. William first worked for William Collins in London, where he became a Creative Director in their paperback division before taking a sabbatical to make a 4,000 mile trek across Europe (France-The Alps-Italy, to Greece) along the old mule tracks, footpaths and pilgrim's routes. Inspired by Patrick Leigh Fermor's *A Time of Gifts*, and Laurie Lee's *As I Walked Out One Midsummer Morning*. On reaching Greece, his original plan was to then head south and walk up the Nile but he believes his better judgement prevailed and returned on a bicycle via North Africa, Spain and France.

For the past thirty years he has built up Goldeneye compiling the research, editorial and photography for more than two hundred UK travel guides and books; on cycling, touring and walking. For many years the Cotswold Hills were William's base. He played cricket in many of the villages, visited many a hostelry and introduced his young family to the wonders of nature. More recently he has been re-developing his Guidebook series to The Cotswolds, Cornwall, Devon and The Lake District.